Alexa

The Ultimate 2018 Step By Step Guide To Master Amazon Alexa

Leonard Eddison

3

This page intentionally left blank

Table of Contents

CHAPTER ONE

Alexa is a service from amazon.com that proposes to audit the traffic received by millions of sites over the internet, over periods of 3 months statistics. To do so, Alexa counts unique visitors on the main page along the day, and then attribute a rank to the site based exclusively on that count. The lower the site rank is, the better classified is the site.

Alexa.com belongs to Amazon and will provide information on the traffic levels to your sites or blogs.

It only measures those sites that have an Alexa toolbar installed. Therefore it really is only a gauge or indicative of your traffic - so use it as such, not as the total be and end of all measurements. It's really a snapshot if that helps you.

Still, it is worthwhile as many advertisers, or those wanting to buy a site, use it as a measure of worth.

As such, it has become, despite its limitations, a primary element in site monetisation strategies.

It measures the traffic you are getting to your website - but it is not 100% accurate, but probably accurate enough to show whether your are improving or not.

The progress is given a score - or numerical number. The lower the number the better your site is.

For example, 1,250,00 is better than 2,350,870. The measure is taken over the last 3 months.

You know you site is good when you are below 100,000 on the Alexa rankings scale.

Why Use It?

1. It shows whether your site is improving - based on the number of visitors

2. You can use it to see the ranking of a competitor - and if his Alexa ranking is lower than yours - it is worth your time to check him out and see if you can discern why - and then copy his tactics.

7

For example: he may have loads more backlinks and is displayed on Google page one. While this may tell you that you need more backlinks, it may also be because his keywords are better.

There are any number of apps available that will help you assess your sites performance. I use them occasionally just to get an indication of where my sites are at.

However, with the proviso, that none I have found give totally accurate information. A simple comparison between them soon reveals this.

Some Ways to Improve Your Alexa Standing
I have garnered these from various sites I have researched, so I don't have personal evidence on all them as to their efficacy.

1. Install the Alexa Toolbar
2. Include an Alexa rank widget onto your website
3. Recommend that others install Alexa

4. Write in your blog - or even on a page on your website about Alexa

5. There are a lot of Asian sites in the top 500 Alexa rankings - they are really into Alexa - so, if and when you have time, explore posting in Asian social networks.

6. Construct a webmasters tool page - and you may find webmasters visiting (and recommending) as they love to get them,

7. This is one I have neglected and should do more of - utilise StumbleUpon and Digg. It does need that you have good material for linking.

To some extent the above are artificial means of increasing your Alexa ranking so it's good to remember nothing really beats developing quality and informative content.to attract an interested audience.

What is sure is that most do require more than set and forget - that is you will have to be regular or consistent in implementing them

Indicative Only

Don't be overly fussed about site and page rankings - if you are regularly adding quality content and doing good SEO, then you will steadily rise in PR and down in Alexa.

CHAPTER TWO

IFTTT

Social Media Management

This type of tools generally allows for the monitoring of social media channels. Marketers can schedule the time of posting for online content. They also provide analytics for the best time for posting on their pages, allowing users to maximize their content reach.

Most managers provide support for sites such as:

- Facebook
- Twitter
- LinkedIn

- Google+
- WordPress
- Instagram
- YouTube

Some of the current widely used tools are:

Hootsuite - currently the most popular management tool. This all-around tool has features such as

- Scheduling,
- Photo attaching,
- Link shortening, and
- Responding to content in hootsuite

However, despite its widespread use, newcomers to Hootsuite may be overwhelmed by its dashboard and may find it unfriendly to users at first glance.

Buffer - specializes more in scheduling and publishing content compared to Hootsuite. It connects all social media profiles together for more streamlined scheduling. One significant difference between Buffer and Hootsuite is that Buffer does not allow its users to respond to comments on their posts.

IFTTT - allows automate sharing. For example, if a writer publishes a new article on their site, an update is automatically posted on the site of their choice. This can enhance both Hootsuite and Buffer experiences.

Sharing Button plugins

Sharing Button plugins are widgets that allow readers to immediately share any interesting posts they find onto their profiles.

It is a subtler way of promoting an article in contrast to posting updates on social media after every new created content.

Many share button plugins also have customization, share tracking, and mobile display optimization features.

Some of the most well-known and affordable plugins are:

- ShareSumo
- Social Warfare
- Monarch
- AddThis
- ShareThis
- Link Shorteners

Aside from their self-explanatory definition, most link shorteners also provide basic analytics. This allowing marketers to monitor which posts on social media have more impact than others. Some also have a monetization feature.

Bitly API - the most well known URL shortener, known for it bit,ly and j.mp extensions.

Short.st API - Features a monetization system, allowing marketers to earn money when users click on links. The downside to this is that the links look like spam.

Sniply - creates call-to-actions to shortened links (CTA), but the free version is limited to 1000 clicks per month only. It also does not feature conversion tracking.

Owly - Hootsuite's built-in link shortener, but has no other features aside from shortening URLs.

IFTTT

Pronounced like gift without the 'G', IFTTT is a innovative new app that stands for "if this than that."

IFTTT provides users with a tool to mix up custom "recipes" that trigger a particular action. Sound confusing?It's not.

The average IFTTT recipe contains the following elements:

Channels: Facebook, Twitter, Instagram, Evernote, iOS photos, Weather, Dropbox, Email, Feedly, iOS Reminders, LinkedIn and 70 more.

Triggers: "I upload a photo to Instagram", "I'm tagged in a photo on Facebook", "I set an iOS reminder"

Actions: "Send me a text message", "Add it to my Dropbox", "Post to Facebook"

Let's say you want to keep your branding consistent across the board, and you want your

Twitter avatar to match your Facebook profile photo. Simply use this "recipe":

If my Facebook profile pictures changes, then update my Twitter profile picture.

A lot of the time when I am working on a "how-to" blog post I reference screenshots from my phone. Oh, you do too? Use this recipe:

If I take a screenshot on iOS, then save it to my Evernote notebook.

With seemingly endless combinations, IFTTT provides busy marketers with a way to automate simple tasks that save a lot of time.

IFTTT is a free web based service (If This Then That) that comes handy by automating your tasks in the Google Drive.

IFTTT's UI is easy because it contains automations or recipes created by users. These can be altered according to your requirements. You can easily alter or copy them as per your convenience. For example, you want to store your tweets in a CSV format on your drive. For this, you need to launch Twitter and give permission to IFTTT for accessing tweets. After this, you need to adjust and authorize IFTTT to send your tweets to the drive

CHAPTER THREE

ALEXA MOST HELPFUL FEATURE

How does Alexa get its data?

Alexa has a large traffic data panel consisting of millions of people all over the world. Based on the data from this sample, Alexa estimates the number of visitors to all sites on the Internet. It's a complicated calculation that involves correcting for biases as well as identifying and discarding fake or spam traffic.

How is the Alexa Ranking determined?

It is based on the amount of traffic recorded from users that have the Alexa toolbar installed over a period of three months. This traffic is based on parameters such as reach and page views. The reach refers to the number of Alexa users who visit a particular site in one day. Page view is the number of times a particular page (URL) is viewed by Alexa users. If a particular user visits the same URL multiple times on the same day, all those visits will be counted as one. There are limits to statistics based on the data available. Sites with relatively low measured traffic will not be accurately ranked by Alexa. Enough data from the sources are not received to make rankings beyond 100,000 statistically meaningful. This means that, for example, the difference in traffic between a site ranked 1,000,000 and a site ranked 2,000,000 has low statistical significance. Sites ranked 100,000+ may be subject to large ranking swings due to the scarcity of data for those sites. It is not unusual for such sites to decline to "No data" Traffic Ranks, or to improve suddenly.

With Alexa, the smaller the numerical ranking, the better.

What are the advantages of Alexa rank?

1. Alexa ranking can be used as a competitive tool to know the traffic for other websites.

2. It helps Webmasters and advertisers see the true marketing potential of your Web site. The better your Alexa rank, the higher they will be willing to bid to buy advertising space on your Web site.

3. Showcasing your traffic statistics and true audience size can help you attract potential customers.

4. Lesser your Alexa ranking is, the better quality traffic you can get.

5. Personal pages or blogs are taken into consideration and ranked in the same manner as regular Web sites. They will even get a distinctive mark (*).

6. Alexa Certified Metrics only counts real traffic. They filter out web crawlers and other unnecessary "noise" which can artificially inflate your metrics. This provides you a clear picture of your true traffic metrics, allowing you to make better business decisions based on genuine data.

7. Alexa Certified Metrics makes performance tracking easy by continually monitoring your site's uptime. They display your uptime next to your traffic graphs allowing you to cross-correlate traffic trends with your site's availability and technical issues.

How to Make your Alexa Rank Better

1. Installing Alexa toolbar in your browser.This the first and the foremost step.

2. Put Alexa widget in your site. This will encourage your visitor to click that.

3. Showcase your Alexa rank to your social media friends/ bloggers friends and link back to your blog.

4. Writing quality and original content. Update the content frequently that provides real value to your audience.Content that drifts from this motivation fails to build quality audiences. When readers find resources valuable and informative, they engage with future content and share among their networks which in turn help in link building. Introducing new visitors that potentially turn into customers.

5. Get more related sites to link to your website that is inbound links. This helps improve the trust and quality of your site. Internal links, on the other hand, are links that lead from one page or post on your site to another. These are beneficial because they guide visitors through your website (i.e. website

navigation), keeping them engaged with relevant and related content.

6. Analysing your competitors marketing strategies and find keywords that are gaining your competitors a better traffic. By doing a little keyword research you can understand what your audiences are searching for and how.

7. Writing articles on Alexa will help to link your page.

8. Making quality backlinks for your site (leaving your website URL in the comment section of the website) which gains good traffic for your site.

9. Follow the best practices of SEO. SEO is a very significant strategy that deserves a substantial amount of your time and attention. But SEO is not just about improving the promotion and visibility of your website. It's also about making your site better for your customers who use it to interface with your

brand. Without a good user experience you have little hope of keeping or converting your customers.

10. Sign up for a free account on Alexa.com and submit your site there.

11. Gain traffic from social media by actively participating in social bookmarking, Micro blogging, Forum and Blog commenting

Want to sell your website and get the most money for it?Or maybe you would like to augment your website's income by selling advertising on it? Or you just want to get a good feel for how well your search engine optimization efforts are working. Then you need to know about Alexa Rankings.

Like it or not (and many people are highly critical of the rankings), Alexa Rankings are the most frequently used statistic to evaluate a site's popularity and traffic. Unlike Google's PageRank, which only evaluates specific webpage's, Alexa Traffic Rankings apply to an entire website.

Alexa's Traffic Rankings come as a function of what Alexa calls "reach", as well as their calculated "page views". Both statistics come from data supplied by users who have the Alexa Toolbar installed. Alexa indicates that over 10 Million people have downloaded their toolbar. Downloading the Alexa Toolbar has appeal since it includes a popup blocker (long before the major browsers did) as well as a search engine entry box, links to both Amazon and Alexa, and the Alexa information about a site.

After the reach (percent of users accessing the site), and page views (number of unique pages accessed by a user during one day), the Traffic Rankings are calculated and Alexa's list of most popular sites is created. The site with the highest ranking is listed as #1, the second highest is #2 and so on.

Criticism of the Alexa Toolbar and Alexa Rankings arise from the Toolbar's intrusive, privacy-breaking toolbar and the Alexa Rankings' bias.Indeed, some spyware programs flag the Toolbar as problematic.

Bias of the Rankings comes from the fact that the data only comes from users of the Toolbar. While the Toolbar exists for the Internet Explorer, Mozilla Firefox and Netscape browsers, and for users of Windows, Macintosh and Linux, some notable Internet users are not -- such as users of the AOL/Netscape browser.

It's commonly, but incorrectly, thought that bias occurs because the Toolbar is only available for Internet Explorer. Even before Alexa came out with their own Toolbar for Firefox, other Firefox extensions existed that provided the same data collection function.

However, it's unknown how many people actually use the Toolbar. The Wikipedia article on the Alexa

24

Toolbar references a 2003 forum posting estimating the actual number of Toolbar users at 180,000.

While some have talked about the Alexa Rankings being a statistical sampling like TV's Nielsen Ratings, perhaps the only thing they have in common is that they are both samplings, and larger estimations of popularity are based upon those samplings. Nielsen, in the finest tradition of polling and statistical sampling, carefully selects their "Neilson homes". Alexa not only does not do this, the users self-select themselves.

Additionally, Alexa indicates that any Alexa Ranking below 100,000 is unreliable, as is any site with fewer than 1000 visitors per month. According to Alexa, "the more traffic a site receives (the closer it gets to the number 1 position), the more reliable its Traffic Ranking becomes."

Ken Evoy, founder of the website building and hosting company Site Build It!, extols the virtues of

Alexa Rankings, in spite of admitting that there is a great deal of "scatter". That is, it's quite possible that a site with only 20 visitors a day might have an Alexa Ranking of 150,000, and a site with 5000 visitors a day with a Ranking of 500,000. He bases his appreciation on the Alexa Rankings that 62% of his customers have been able to achieve traffic rankings within the top 3%.

So, how can you increase your Alexa Traffic Rank? Most obviously, get more traffic. This can be done by search engine optimization (SEO) efforts as well as by a myriad of other traffic-generating strategies.

However, you can also bump your Ranking by taking advantage of Alexa Ranking weaknesses. For instance, encourage all your website visitors to download and install the Alexa Toolbar. Visit your own website! Alexa doesn't know it's your website, so has no way of eliminating this bias. There are also a number of software tools and scripts that can bemused, ranging from $49 to free (alexabooster is a popular one), to code written into forum postings.

In order to improve your Alexa standing, you need to increase traffic to your website.

Installing the Alexa Tool Bar:

By installing the Alexa toolbar on your browser, and encouraging your friends and colleagues to do so as well, you can boost your Alexa rating.

Claiming your website:

Go to Alexa dot com and claim your website. By doing this, you are letting others know who owns the website. In turn it will boost your rating.

Placing the Alexa Widget On Your Blog:

The Alexa widget will help boost your rating.

Blog About Alexa:

Write a review about Alexa Ranking and link back to Alexa.com.

Know Alexa's Target Audience:

By knowing Alexa's target audience and what they are searching for, you can write about those topics to boost your Alexa rating. Webmasters and social media experts who make their livelihood marketing to the web typically have the Alexa toolbar installed on their browsers. Create good Search Engine Optimized (SEO) content to entice these readers to your website.

Backlinking and Commenting:

Backlinking your content to others who have written similar content will increase the overall value of your content to a search engine. Also, commenting on public forums and referencing your article will also increase the value of your page. Search Engine Optimization is an organic way to get more people to visit your site.

Blog Regularly:

In order to increase your Alexa rating, you must blog regularly, ideally three times a week.

Post Quality Work:

The quality of your posts matter. If your work is well thought out and crafted well, others will link back to you, which will increase your Alexa rating.

Utilize Social media:

Sharing your posts through various social media outlets will bring more traffic to your website. By increasing your website's traffic, you will be increasing your Alexa rating.

Purchase Traffic:

There are a number of sites where you can buy website traffic. While not generally recommended, because the traffic is short lived and transient, in the short term, this can be a very effective way to boost your Alexa rating

Analysis on Some Features of Alexa

For people who would like to boost Alexa rank, attention here. Alexa, one of the biggest website ranking tools, has quietly added some analysis functions for source keywords, visitors' actions, age,

sex and occupation, and even whether they have
children.

Alexa has been revised before so as to provide the
average period of stay per person per day, enquiry
function of curve graph showing average PV per
person, and enquiry function of return visit of regular
customers.

Taking search results on 'Baidu' as an example:

(The most frequently appearing keyword pointing
to Baidu website from search engines)

We can see that:

1) A lot of people inputted in the search engines
the Chinese phonetic alphabets for 'Baidu', most
likely by using a third-party browser or plug-in;

2) MP3 is still one of the biggest advantages of
Baidu;

3) Baidu contributes huge traffic to QQ;

4) RSS and perpetual calendar are very popular.

From analysis on visitor's action sequence, we can
draw the following conclusions:

1) Between Baidu and Google, 3.93% of the visitors would take Google as the first choice, while 2.87% preferred Baidu;

2) Information on portal websites, video and search engines are still the favorite of visitors;

3) 1.66% of visitors got access through web address guide, which indicates that web address guide has relatively stable market.

From analysis on visitor's age, sex, occupation and whether they have children, we may see that:

1) The data are somewhat unreasonable; they can only be used for reference;

2) Alexa might go on to develop follow-up analysis functions, such as how much the monthly income of the visitor is.

And the list of the websites whose Alexa ranks are less than 100,000, with PR value, is provided. The revision makes some data of each website more transparent.When you are analyzing your competitors, you are also analyzed by them. This is a reform of Alexa.

If you want to increase Alexa rank, you'd better have a study on the tool. Some people may consider Alexa rank of no use, well however, we have to admit that Alexa does hold the third rank in the world's biggest website ranking institutions. If you need to demonstrate the value of your website, Alexa rank can be a significant indicator, especially when you want to sell your website or sell links and ads on your website, or make the performance report for your company - Alexa rank can add extra points for you in all the conditions. The revision process has just started, and more will be done. Let's see what will Alexa do next?

CHAPTER FOUR

AMAZON ECHO

Amazon Echo Accessories - Do You Need Them?
OK so you might have just bought your Amazon Echo and you might be wondering what kind of accessories are available or how important they are. There is one feature that this gadget has and that is

the ability to turn your lights on or off by voice command or anything else that is plugged in for that matter. That's right, you ask Alexa to turn your lights on or off and that is exactly what she will do.

Through your smart phone she can even turn on the lights as you are driving up to the house. It's not just your garage door you can open when you are driving up to your house anymore.

What Else Can Alexa Turn On and Off?

Turn On Your Space Heater

Coffee Maker

Night Lights

Christmas Lights

Iron (incase you accidentally left it on)

Fans

And much more!

As you can see, if you love convenience, then you will love this particular feature. To enjoy it though you would need the "Wemo Switch and the Wemo Light Bulb".

Hard Leather Cases - Just In Case...

The Amazon Echo also has hard leather cases which I think would be a necessity. Just don't get one that has the appearance of a dog bone and you will be OK.

The one thing I really like about the protective cases is that they have a lot of different designs to make your device really snazzy looking.There are also tons of designs to choose from. I am not sure just how much a leather case would protect your new toy, but they also do have hard case protection as well.

Don't Want To Protect It? Then Skin It

Next up is some eye candy and that is the Skin. This doesn't really fall into the I Need This category, but still is nice to look at. As with the protective leather cases the Amazon Echo skins also have many, many designs. I have read some reviews on these skins and some people have had a hard time getting the wrinkles out once they have put the skins on. I dunno maybe they didn't put them on right as there are not a terrible amount of complaints on this issue.

Wooden Holders...

If you would rather not worry about putting your Amazon Echo in a protective case to stash it away somewhere then you could go with the Amazon Echo Wooden Holder that actually looks pretty darn good.

The Remote Control...

This was a pretty nice accessory to have, but they have been out of stock for some time and Amazon does not know if and when it will be coming back. The Amazon Echo Remote would have allowed you to control your Amazon Echo from any room in the house. I sure hope they are either making more or found whatever issues it was having and fix it so they can bring it back.

Have you heard an Echo lately?

Amazon continues to expand its lineup of Echo products. The company that introduced us to Alexa now has more devices to listen to music, get news and information, and control your smart home all by simply using your voice.

First came the cylinder like Echo.It was followed up by the hockey puck-like Echo Dot.Then Amazon added video into the mix with the Echo Show. Now comes the smaller Echo Spot and the Echo Plus.

For many looking for a virtual home assistant, the question becomes should you buy an Echo and if so which one?

Those who like to watch, as well as listen, should take a front-row type look at the Echo Show.

The Show enables you to watch video flash briefings, Amazon Video and YouTube content, and make video calls to family and friends.All on a 7 inch touch screen.

You can see music lyrics, weather forecasts and your security cameras. Even create your own to-do and shopping lists.

Navigation is easy by swiping left or right. The screen also recommends some commands for Alexa if you don't know what to ask.

The 1024 x 600 screen is nearly identical to the one on the Amazon Fire 7 tablet. The text is legible but not as crisp as your smartphone or television.

The touch screen enables you to adjust settings and brightness levels. You can change a lot of things without using the Alexa app or mobile device.

In addition to the 7 inch screen the Show includes a 5 megapixel camera.

The device has an angular design. Some find it a bit clunky and liken it to a triangle with two shaved points when you look at it from the side. Overall it measures 7 x 7.4 x 4 inches and has a square foot panel facing at an angle that is slightly upward.

Eight microphones with noise cancellation are included. Amazon says you can issue commands from any direction, even while music is playing.

Like all of the Echo line you can stream music, turn on lights, set thermostats and control other compatible smart home devices.

It is easy to use. Once you plug it in it will show you available Wi-Fi networks. Pick a network and log into your Amazon account and you are ready to go.

Speakers include two, 2 inch speaker drivers for stereo audio powered by Dolby.

The Bluetooth capabilities are what many are finding as the real selling point of this device. Functioning as a Bluetooth speaker, as well as a sound source, you can pair the Show with your smartphone or tablet and play music through its speaker. You can use it with a separate Bluetooth speaker or headphones and stream audio directly out of the device itself.

Shopping is easier with the Show than with the voice only devices. Alexa adds items directly into your Amazon shopping cart and even places instant orders. The touch screen allows you to swipe through products if you cannot identify the actual product you want. However you won't be able to check your cart with the Show. You will need a computer to view or edit your cart and/or place your entire order.

Amazon continues to add more "skills" to the Alexa ecosystem such as Uber and CNN, and newer apps with more video capabilities are on the way.

Yet the Echo Show does have its limitations. While the addition of video certainly enhances the Alexa experience, sound quality may not be up to par on all music. The quality of voice and video calls are not up to the standards of Google Hangouts and Skype. Applications are limited by the Alexa-specific system.

Still the device is ideally suited for those wishing to join the ranks of Echo users or for those current fans who wish to take the Alexa experience to the next level. And now, at newly reduced prices, the Echo Show may just be the way to go.

TECHNOLOGIES CAN HELP ANYONE TO GET THE BEST OUT OF DOING YOGA AND MEDITATION AT HOME.

1) Practise "Stop, Breathe, Think" with Amazon Alexa

Amazon's voice-controlled smart home assistant is called Alexa. There are many different devices available now that Amazon has launched featuring Alexa. They include the Amazon Echo (a larger speaker for playing music) and the Amazon dot, which is a smaller version without the large speaker but can still hear you and respond to commands.Alexa has thousands of different useful skills which can be activated just with a voice command. There is a whole section of skills in the Health & Fitness category, one of which is the "Stop, Breathe, Think" skill. You can say "Alexa, open Stop, Breathe, Think" and one of various meditation routines will be activated. The calm and relaxing voice will lead you through a guided meditation as opposed to you trying to clear your busy mind alone in a silent room.

There are two primary reasons digital assistants haven't taken off on mobile platforms -

Using voice commands is just plain awkward in public places and public places is where people mostly use their phone.

If one were to pull their phone and push a button before they can talk to their phone, they might as well push that extra button and see what is on the calendar instead of asking the assistant.

Amazon, a company which largely played a 'me-too' role in consumer product space had a totally different take on voice assistants. They dreamed of and came up with a new product category altogether when they launched Echo - an always on, cloud powered voice assistant for home.

Echo (also called Alexa) was designed by Amazon to be a product that stays at home because Amazon figured that voice assistants are best suited for home usage. This is evident by the fact that they didn't even bother to put a battery in it which is a bold move in today's world of mobile gadgets. Then they made it insanely easy to get Echo's attention. You just wake her up with a wake word (Alexa or Amazon are the only supported wake words for now) and then issue whatever command you want. Echo comes with seven sensitive microphones and can hear you from more than 10 feet away even in a noisy room. It can hear you even when it is playing music or talking to you. By removing the two major hurdles listed above, Amazon created a voice assistant that is actually useful and fun to use.

Like a phone that can do a whole bunch of things by installing apps, Echo can be used for many purposes too. It can play music, answer trivia, control smart devices, set alarms, manage calendars etc. I often hear people questioning the utility of Echo because their phone can do pretty much everything Echo can do.That was my first reaction to the product too but once I started using Echo, it slowly got on to me. I understood the power of an always connected voice assistant that I can just talk to from anywhere in the house without having to push any buttons.

Take setting a timer while cooking, for example. Previously, I would have to wash my hands, dry them, pull my phone, activate Siri and ask her to set a timer. She would do it and when the timer goes off, I would hear a faint sound on my iPhone's tiny speakers. Compare that to the convenience of just saying 'Alexa, set a timer for 30 seconds' and getting a notification that can be heard all over the house (yes, Echo comes with very good speakers). Once you get used to the freedom and convenience Echo offers, using a smart phone feels like an ordeal and every other digital assistant feels like they are from 1970s.

This is not to say Echo is the dream AI product from the future. It does manage to annoy you quite a bit sometimes by not being able to answer basic questions and not responding to you in a loud room. Echo's ability to answer general trivia questions is fairly limited.

To conclude, I think Amazon finally figured out how to make digital assistants useful and if you are one of those people who are skeptical about its usefulness, I would strongly recommend trying Echo for a little while and you would realize how inferior every other digital assistant is. Sure it can annoy you once in a while but you would eventually learn to start living with her. In fact, I liked mine so much that I bought a second Echo for my bed room.

Battery Boots: The Alternative Power Source For The Amazon Echo

The Amazon Echo touted as a bestselling voice activated wireless speaker and personal digital assistant. Most owners of this device use it for more than listening to music or asking interesting questions and requests. Other applications include being able to obtain transportation, order a pizza and the ability to control integrated smart devices inside their home.

According to the Consumer Intelligence Research Partners (CIRPs), it estimates that 3 million units of the Amazon Echo were sold in the United States. The data does not account for the sales of the new additions to the line, the Tap and Echo Dot. Novelty aside, the Echo is growing in popularity on a daily basis. The reviews of the device are above average, while the benefits are even more surprising.

Amazon is one of the leaders in digital media, but it didn't have any idea how well consumers would receive the Echo. It started out being a sleeper item until word of mouth made it a household name and not to mention, the recent appearance of commercials showing off its neat features.

The "skills" utilized by the device through the digital assistant are updated periodically and now open to outside developers to add their innovative and well-meaning list of skills for more technological enhancement. Because of the Echo is the first of its kind so to speak, they have competitors clamoring for their piece of the pie. Such as Google Home, which will have a better interactive interface and then, of course, the re-emergence of Apple TV.

The number of consumers that own the Echo is quite impressive. However, some have complained about the cost and the inconvenience of having to move it from room to room. To address these issues, Amazon introduced two additional Echo models.

The Tap, which is the portable version of the speaker, does not need to be plugged in unless the battery is being recharged. It functions the same as the Echo, but is not voice activated. The talk button has to be pressed for interaction with the device, thus the name Tap. The other new member is the Echo Dot. It is as small as a hockey-puck but has the same voice activation as the Echo. A Bluetooth speaker or stereo system can be connected to it.

I own an Echo, but for it to work efficiently, there must be a Wi-Fi connection and electricity. Without either, it will not function. Because of the need for electricity, some consumers have taken to purchasing one for each room in their house. It saves them time from having to move it from room to room and waiting for it to reboot once it is plugged into an electric outlet.

Some consumers debated whether to purchase the Tap since it's portable. However, lucky for them they procrastinated, because a few third party vendors have introduced a new accessory for the Echo, a battery boot or base.

It is now possible to enjoy the device in more than one room without having to be tethered to an electric outlet. However, there is still a need for a Wi-Fi or Bluetooth connection. There are several battery boots to choose from according to the needs of the user. The more popular model has its own 18-volt proprietary power adapter that will charge up to 18 hours.

There are other battery boots that can hold a charge for up to six hours. For these models, the Echo's power adapter cord can be used to recharge them. The Echo can be used while it is charging. The battery will remain in a standby state, so it does not drain while plugged in.

The bases fit snugly on the bottom of the Echo like a cup and does not present a bulky appearance. Both devices appear to meld together once fitted properly. The bottom of the boots is composed of non-slip materials that provide stability for the Echo.

A couple of the battery bases have LED lights on the front for low battery and charging status. Portability and convenience make these battery cases a welcome power alternative option for the Amazon Echo.

High Tech Home Automation Upgrades

Bring your home into the 21st century with some high tech home automation upgrades.

Many people have already advanced their property with home automation upgrades, but may be completely unaware that they have. You may already use products such as the Nest thermostat or the Amazon Echo, these products are in fact technologies that are part of the home automation revolution that is changing the way people live in their homes.

Today's market provides a home automation device for each and every room in your home. Below are some of the top home automation products to upgrade your home.

In the kitchen

Bluetooth thermometer

You will never mistakenly burn your meal again with a helpful smart meat thermometer. It works by sending the information from the thermometer to your smart phone via a Bluetooth connection, showing you when your pork, chicken, turkey, or fish reaches the right temperature.

Slow cooker

You can start dinner before you leave the office with a Wi-Fi enabled crock pot. By simply swiping your finger across your smart phone you can turn the cooker on, set the temperature, or turn it off to make sure that your dinner isn't burnt if you are delayed in getting back to your home.

Wi-Fi enabled kettle

Set the kettle to boil remotely by using an app on your smart phone. Whether you want the kettle to be boiled before you get out of bed or ready for you when you get home from work, the Wi-Fi enabled iKettle will boil your water and even hold its temperature for up to a half hour.

In the bathroom

Bluetooth speakers for the shower

Sing along to your favorite songs with the Aqua-tunes waterproof speaker and add some entertainment to your home automation upgrades. The speaker connects to your phone or tablet via Bluetooth and enables you to stream music from your device that is played in the shower. Simply hook the speaker on to your shower rod and press the sync button to link up with your mobile device.

Heated toilet seat

LumaWarm offer the heated nightlight toilet seat. The seat is illuminated by a blue LED light and is equipped with multiple temperature settings that warm the seat within a couple of minutes.

In the bedroom

Smart bedroom lighting

Smart lighting can help you relax at the end of the day, and even help you fall asleep, with lighting that is personalized to you, with dimming and variable color temperatures. There are several types of smart lighting products available for home automation upgrades, with some set by timers that can be easily accessed and changed through your smart phone, while others utilize motion sensors to adapt the lighting to your nightly routine.

Smart windows

Equip your windows with smart window film, or adjustable blinds that operate by a motor, which can be accessed on your smart phone. Smart blinds and shades can adapt and respond to the lighting level outside and are a must for your home automation upgrades. Smart window film offers the ability to transition your window from clear to opaque by simply tapping a button on your smart phone.

Home automation for any room

Smart sockets/plugs

Smart plugs are a simple and easy way to make a start upgrading your home. The smart socket device plugs into your existing power outlet and enables you to remotely control the power usage and keep an eye on your energy usage.

Humidity detector

The Humidity Sensor and Fan Control by Leviton can identify the level of humidity in your home and automatically react to it by turning on a ventilation fan. The smart device can be used in the bathroom and any other area of your home to reduce moisture in the air.

Room by room upgrades

If you still don't really know where to start with your home automation upgrades, there are several home automation upgrades and smart home upgrade kits on the market.

The main purpose of home automation upgrades is to make daily tasks easier for the user. You don't need to rush and try to upgrade everything in your home at once. Identify areas of your home or exact tasks where you would appreciate some technological help, then research what home automation options are available to fulfill your needs.

CHAPTER FIVE

CONNECT YOUR GO=GLE CALENDER AND
PANDORA ACCOUNT TO ALEXA

Virtual assistants like Amazon's Alexa are
becoming more and more integrated into our daily
lives. Recently, Google released their competitor to
Amazon's product. Aptly named, Google Home, the
Google Home Assistant can help you in surprising
ways you might not have realized at first. Here are 15
features that might surprise you.

1. Use It as a Speaker

It's common knowledge that it comes equipped
with a Bluetooth speaker. However, it's not limited
to just connecting to your phone and playing
playlists. It can connect to many music streaming
services, like Spotify and Pandora. Not only that but
with an integrated chrome browser on any
computer, you can easily connect your computer to
it and use it as a desktop speaker.

2. Read the News from 1851

It has a database of news headlines going back all the way to 1851. All you have to do is ask for the news on any specific day. It will then read the headlines of that day and summarizes the news contained in that article.

3. Find Your Phone

With just a simple phrase, Google Home Assistant can place a call to your phone to help you find it. If your phone is on silent or vibrate and is compatible with Google Home, it will even come out of silent mode in order for you to hear its ring.

4. Turn Your Lights On or Off

It is advertised as the central hub for all your smart devices. If you have compatible lights such as the Phillips Hue bulbs, then you can ask it to turn off and on the lights for you without pressing a switch.

5. Use Touch Commands

It is equipped with touch-sensitive technology that knows where your fingers are and can register many gestures. You can tap the top to pause and unpause music and sliding your finger to the side opens up the volume control. Google has promised more functionality of touch commands in the future.

6. Get an Uber

By connecting your Uber app to Google Home and specifying a few settings, you can ask it for an Uber and one will go right to your house in a matter of minutes.

7. Cook Recipes

Perhaps one of the most useful functions, it can look up over five million recipes via several databases such as the New York Time and Food Network. The Google Home Assistant will go through the recipe step by step and you can even ask it for conversions and ingredient substitutions.

8. Play 20 Questions

It is connected to Akinator, which is an online version of 20 questions. You simply think of something, and Akinator, via Google Home will ask questions to narrow it down. It's perfect for when you are bored or want to keep your kids occupied.

9. Keep a Shopping List

Google Home has a lot of functionality in the kitchen. If you notice you're missing something, simply ask Google Assistant to add the item to your shopping list. That shopping list is automatically sent to any integrated phone or smart device.

10. Integrate With Chromecast

If you have Chromecast, Google's home TV option, then you can use Google Home and voice commands to control it. You can ask for specific videos, or tell it to rewind, forward, or skip to a specific time.

11. Know Your Traffic

By adding your home and work locations to its app, the Google Home Assistant can tell you about traffic conditions and possible alternate routes you can take to save time.

12. Impress Your Guests

It allows your guests to use it as well. All they have to do is pair their device with Google Home, a step that literally takes seconds. Once it is paired, they can issue commands and ask questions just as you can.

13. See Your Pics on TV

It can be given access to your photo accounts, like Google Photo and Photobucket. Once you do, you can use Chromecast to show your pictures on TV and even ask for specific pictures based on location and date.

14. Relax

It comes with over 15 ambient sounds, including forest ambiance and crashing waves, to help you relax or fall asleep.

15. Hear a Joke

It can even tell jokes. Just ask, and you shall receive.

With all these things you can do with Google Home and more features added soon, now is a great time to buy this fantastic home assistant

CHAPTER SIX

ALEXA TOOLBARS

For many of us, life on the web is not complete without referring time and again to one or more toolbars. Near to 60% of all web-users I've visited thus far have their browsers sporting trendy toolbars, most commonly Google toolbar. As ubiquitous as they may be, we all have personal choice of toolbars like branded items, though it seems only a handful are more popular over a wide cross-section of surfers.

But, what is a toolbar?

Most often a toolbar is like a main menu-bar residing alongside in popular browsers, usually Microsoft's Internet Explorer. Like browser's menu-bar, a toolbar too provides many options to viewers, the main aim being bringing focus to surfing on the net. Various hues of toolbars are available, majority of them being free of cost, but one feature that is common in nearly all of them is the ability to easily browse for relevant information from respective search engine. A second feature found in most toolbars is blocking pop-up and pop-under ad, which of late has proved to be more of an irritant than help.

How does toolbar fit in?

For people who frequently surf the net for information, a toolbar is of great help. The world-wide-web contains wealth of information ready to be tapped for use.Yet, for many, getting precise information is more often than not a frustrating experience. If you happen to refer to this book, titled "Google Power: Unleash the Full Potential of Google" [http://www.amazon.com/gp/product/0072257873/] by Chris Sherman, you would know that to get right information would rather require practiced skill so as to formulate your query perfectly. That is to say, if you're not pretty skilled to do your searches, you may in all probability need to fine-tune your searches again and again. And this is where the toolbars come as great help. Toolbars do not eliminate pain of searching. It instead assists in pruning your browsing time so that you can devote more time to do what you want to with the information collected.

A subtle difference can be made out in the working of various toolbars. Thus, while search toolbars allow searching in your favorite search engines directly, meta search utilities are for searching multiple search engines simultaneously.

Alexa toolbar - how it helps?

One of my favorites is Alexa Toolbar. The variety of information that can be culled from Alexa toolbar about any webpage (and of course a website) is truly amazing. Alexa owes it to millions of users of its toolbar, for 2 of the most important toolbar information (Related Links and Traffic rankings) are basically aggregated culminations of what its toolbar users do while surfing the net.

But first, let us go through Alexa toolbar's main features and how they're helpful to web-surfers like you and me.

Traffic rank at-a-glance

The most impressive is perhaps the unique at-a-glance traffic ranking of any website. The figure displayed denotes the traffic rank of a particular website. Remember this is not the actual traffic rank. This figure is just a reflection of where a particular website is positioned in the long queue of those websites that are visited by users of Alexa toolbar. Now, if you feel this ranking is flawed, so it is. No doubt there. Yet, many people rely on this figure for the simple reason that in absence of any other similar data, Alexa toolbar users do form a good sample (even if insignificant compared to total web population) to provide some basic unbiased information.

Links to similar websites

The second very useful information that can be had from Alexa toolbar are links to some more websites that are similar to the one being presently viewed. A great help that. Why? Suppose you are looking for information on, say mosquito repellent. You start by searching the term on your favorite search engine, which then throws up a list of urls' closely matching your search term in the SERP (search engine result page). As you select a url from the list and browse the related website that deals on the subject of your search term, you will simultaneously be shown links on the toolbar of similar other websites. If you feel the current webpage or website is not up to your expectation or if you are inclined to explore more options, you may simply click on the link of a similar other website shown on the toolbar.

When you follow one of those links and visit the new site, 2 things happen. One is of course that you are able to view a similar website without much of an effort. Second is that you will get to see a new set of related links on the toolbar that may be partially or fully same or different from the earlier ones. You will thus have multiple options of websites while you roam from one site to another looking for required information without the hassle of repeatedly referring to search engines. This feature allows you to save time you would have otherwise spent for searching afresh. Isn't that a topper? You bet.

What else?

Quite a lot. For example, you will know 'reach' of your website per million toolbar users, which other sites link to yours (pretty common feature), search in various platforms (like stocks, news, dictionary and thesaurus, default search being in Google), email a webpage to your friend, be quickly taken to Amazon (Alexa is an Amazon company) for shopping and so on.

But what perhaps takes the cake is the feature provided in collaboration with WayBackMachine [http://www.archive.org/web/web.php], said to be the largest internet archive online. When you click the link (toward the right end of the toolbar, the 'page history') you will be taken to WayBackMachine's search result page that details year-wise links of your website since the time it has come online. You click a link that says say 'April 12, 1999', and pronto you get to see what your website looked then. I felt pretty nostalgic while recently checking my painting website. Like seeing my childhood pictures in half-pants, eh! To download Alexa toolbar, click here [http://download.alexa.com/index.cgi].

Not for Firefox

Well then, an Alexa toolbar does indeed make web-life easier. There is though a major drawback. Firefox does not allow Alexa toolbar, and so Firefox users will remain bereft of Alexa's advantages.However Firefox does permit using Quirk's SearchStatus [http://www.quirk.biz/searchstatus/], which is quite a useful tool.SearchStatus is basically a toolbar extension for Mozilla and Mozilla Firefox users.

Do you need more?

The answer is a qualified 'yes'. You may also need Google toolbar to make your web-life more complete.Let me explain. If you are an IE user, you may certainly like to install Google toolbar, for how else would you automatically know the PageRank of a webpage! On the other hand, if you make do with Firefox, you may perhaps omit Google toolbar if you have installed Quirk's SearchStatus.

But then Google toolbar is so feature-rich that without it you will miss out on many advantages. I am not going to explain Google toolbar anew.Click here [http://www.google.com/support/toolbar/bin/static.py?page=features.html] to know all you need to. The bottomline therefore is if you are an active surfer, you will most certainly benefit from both Alexa toolbar (or its 'derivative' through SearchStatus) and Google toolbar. As they say if it is good to be informative, it is still better to know how to remain informative. To that extent, toolbars are a necessity on the web, if not must-ha

CHAPTER SEVEN

HOW TO IMPROVED ALEXA RANK AND ITS BENEFITS

Alexa Rank is a scheme of ranking of websites or blogs in which the ranking is done on the basis of the density of traffic every website or blog has by counting the number of visitors at a particular time. But for Alexa Rank to work, it must be ensured that Alexa Toolbar is installed and is running. Installing Alexa Toolbar is recommended because the bloggers and advertising companies or advertising networks such as Sponsored Reviews and Blogvertisers normally pay attention on the Alexa Rank for deciding whether a review be obtained for the said blogs or websites.

High number of Alexa rank of a website seems to be important just because, the advertising companies rely on this ranking to determine the cost for placing advertisements in the concerned websites. Many advertisers and ad networks use Alexa Rank to determine the website's value of advertising, as examples; Text Link Ads, Sponsored Reviews and such advertising companies. Using Alexa Rank, these companies decide how much to pay for an advertisement in the websites or blogs. Hence, higher Alexa Rank gives higher popularity and inclination towards such websites.

Benefits of Higher Alexa Rank

There are many benefits of higher Alexa Rank as; the Alexa Ranking scheme considers records of last three months when calculating the Rank of a particular website. By counting last three months' record and taking the average value, gives a more logical and realistic calculation of the density of traffic of websites. Considering records of last three months lessen the chance of fabrication of abnormal hike in website logging in. Here it must be kept in mind that Alexa assess those web sites which have been visited by the users through the Alexa toolbar. Hence, there are greater chances for web sites which have much traffic of visitors and have higher Alexa rank, to get larger exposure.

Further on the other side, if some websites have few users but through Alexa toolbar they accessed the website and the same website will get ranked high enough. Having higher Alexa rank for a website gives a hint of the rush of a particular web site and the popularity of it. This popularity helps to make a decision as to whether to trust a website or make online purchases. It helps to measure the level of competition with other web sites by watching others' Alexa Rank.

Also, having high Alexa Rank attracts advertisers and they simply fix higher prices for their advertising in your web site. This includes blogs also. A blog which has high Alexa Rank definitely attracts other bloggers attention and they definitely place links of your blogs which in turn increases your popularity.

HOW TO IMPROVE YOUR ALEXA RANKING

Every business wishes to increase its Alexa rank. Basically, it is a website ranking system in which ranking is done on the basis of traffic density at a particular point of time. It is reliable and popular. All you need to do is to install its toolbar. Alexa rank can provide you various monetary benefits as well because advertisers look for this rank to decide the cost of advertisements to be placed on your website or blog. The higher your rank, the more money you make.

Reap Various Benefits

There are various benefits of a high rank. It gives a more realistic estimate of traffic density. This way you can know where your site actually stands. If you want to advertise your business through blogs and websites, you can always select those with high rankings. Also, if you want to make an online purchase, select those merchants who have a good rank. If you own an online shop yourself, you should increase your Alexa ranking to get more customers. You can gauge the level of competition in your field of business by analyzing the alexa rankings of other players. It becomes important therefore to increase your Alexa ranking.

As compared to other ranking systems, a lower rank is the better. When you increase your Alexa ranking, you are actually striving for a lower number. Not just websites, blogs and personal web pages are also taken into consideration. The last two categories get a distinctive mark too. If you improve your Alexa ranking, you can have efficient search engine optimization. This ranking helps a lot in SEO.

COMMON TIPS TO FOLLOW

There are various ways in which you can increase your Alexa ranking. Some commonly followed and highly effective methods are given below:

* Get Alexa Toolbar: It is important to get the tool bar installed to use Apolexa. If you have more than one computer, you can install in all the systems to increase the effect and get good results.

* Alexa Widget: You should put the widget on your blog or website. This will help you in getting the high rank. This widget is easily available and can be installed easily.

* Posts: writing always helps. You can post about Alexa and this way you can tell more people about Alexa thus increasing traffic activity on your site.

The Ranking System

The Alexa rank is calculated by calculating the geometric mean of historical traffic data and page views taken over a period of three months. This way, the rank reflects the user traffic and number of website pages viewed by them. If you want to increase your Alexa ranking, you must download its toolbar as this system can only work through the toolbar.

You can easily know about the health of your business by comparing your rank with other competitors. If it is not good then take measures to increase your Alexa ranking. The top rank is one. The higher the rank, lower the traffic. You should strive for a lower rank. Let's assume the rank of your website of blog or webpage is 524895. This is not at all a good rank as it means the traffic to your site is quite low and there are 524894 sites ahead of you in the parameter of customer visits. You should always try to improve your Alexa ranking.

WAYS TO RAPIDLY IMPROVE YOUR BLOG'S RANK IN ALEXA

1. Install Alexa toolbar and set your blog as the home page. As you know, Alexa rank is determined on the basis of the information collected by the Alexa toolbar. Only the click of the visitor who has it installed will be counted when he visits your website. As the webmaster of a personal website, the first thing you should do is to install it on your own browser and set your blog to be the home page so that every time you open IE, you make a little contribution to your own site for Alexa rank improvement.

2. Install Alexa toolbar on all computers you can touch. And set your blog as the home page. Encourage all people you know to install Alexa toolbar.

3. Put up a Alexa counter widget on your blog. When it is clicked, it will be counted as traffic by Alexa, even if the one who clicks it does not install the Alexa toolbar.

4. Write some articles about Alexa on your blog. You can even open a Alexa column. Many webmasters would like to see these things. If you write good articles, they are likely to republish or link to them, which also can bring you traffic and hence help to increase Alexa rank.

5. Go to where webmasters often visit and post the URL of your blog there. Generally, webmasters have Alexa toolbar installed. You may go to some

webmaster forums to write posts promoting your blog.

6. Tell friends to vote for your blog on Alexa website. Though it is not sure how much this will benefit your blog's Alexa rank, it is better to have a good rating.

7. Write the columns that webmasters would be concerned about, such as an SEO column, to attract more webmasters to visit your site.

8. Use Alexa redirection function.

9. If possible, go to some foreign forums or websites to promote your blog, for foreign surfers often install the Alexa toolbar.

10. If you have sufficient funds, you may consider buying some pay-per-click ads for your blog. That can bring abundant IP.

11. Add links to Alexa relevant content in your most popular articles on your blog, or use Alexa redirection to link to other places of your blog.

12. Buy professional service to boost Alexa rank. Of course it is stable, safe and effect-guaranteed.

ALEXA TRAFFIC RANK

On a daily basis, Alexa collects statistics about the number of visitors and page views for every website on the Internet. Actually, it does not have data for all the sites. You see, data collection happens via web surfers that have downloaded and installed the Alexa toolbar for their Internet Explorer browser. When one of these users visits and explores a site, the toolbar sends this information to Alexa's servers. What this means for webmasters is that only those sites visited by users that have decided to install the toolbar will actually have data collected for them. In addition, since only a rather small subset of all possible Web surfers actually uses the toolbar, the ranking is a statistical average that is not necessarily a true indication of the quality and number of a site's readers. In fact, the number is really inaccurate for sites with a small number of visitors and Alexa admits that this is true for those sites not in the top 100,000.

To make matters worse, the toolbar is only available for Internet Explorer. Of course, IE is the browser used by the majority of Internet users with data showing that it is used by about 83% of them (onestat.com). This is not a problem unless your audience is more likely to be in the other 17% of surfers, i.e., those that prefer to use Firefox, Safari, Opera or another alternative browser. For example, slashdot.org is a technology news site with an audience that is known to be very anti-Microsoft; Slashdot's motto is "News for nerds. Stuff that matters." One expects that most of its users would use any browser other than IE and in fact it was recently posted that an estimated 65% of Slashdot's readers use a browser other than IE. As of this writing (July 12, 2006), Slashdot's ranking was 176 with a reach of 5450 per million surfers. Slashdot is known for something called the "Slashdot effect" that is when a story on the front page links to a site, it receives so many visitors that the servers often are not able to handle the sudden increase in traffic. In other words, I would expect that Alexa's rank is actually an underestimate of Slashdot's true rank.

From a statistics point of view, Alexa's rank cannot be thought of as an unbiased statistical measure. The sample of people used by Alexa for collecting data is not a randomly selected set but rather it is biased towards users of Microsoft Windows and Internet Explorer as well as those who are willing to install the toolbar and submit to Alexa information about their browsing behavior. If your audience is similar to Slashdot's then don't expect accurate results. Anticipate the same if your audience includes people who are pro-privacy and would never install a toolbar that calls home making their browsing behavior known to a large corporation.

So, if you really want accuracy in terms of your site's number of users and page views then you are better off using analytics software, for example Google Analytics, rather than Alexa. However, many advertisers use Alexa's ranking as a neutral third party estimate of a site's popularity; they consult Alexa in order to determine how much advertising space is worth on your site. This is the reason why many webmasters display their Alexa rank on the front page. If you happen to be on the upper end of Alexa's ranking then you should be able to benefit from it; if you are not then you probably shouldn't lose too much sleep over it. Focus on adding fresh content to your site; this way you will be able to drive more traffic to your site via the major search engines and also keep your visitors coming back.

THE VALUE OF ALEX TRAFFIC RANKING FOR WEBMASTERS

The value of the Alexa Traffic Ranking for webmasters should not be underestimated. Firstly, it is the closest thing to a universal, impartial 3rd party measure of traffic we have. It can give webmasters a fair idea of the competition. This is information that the competition will not readily share.

Webmasters looking for new projects can use Alexa Rankings to identify new trends and possibilities. For example, if you followed the Alexa Rankings, you would have had a head's up on the rise of myspace.com and milliondollarhomepage.com.

Domain specialists use Alexa rankings to register domain typos for popular domains and domains which rankings are dramatically rising. Again, sites that are quickly rising in traffic/popularity give domain specialists an idea of the direction the domain market is headed, and they can proactively procure valuable domain names.

Basically any webmaster with an interest in new trends and the rise and fall of certain types of sites, can benefit from Alexa Rankings.

CHAPTER EIGHT

WHY IS ALEXA RANK IMPORTANT TO YOUR SERPS RANK?

Before you come to know the importance of Alexa rank for your SERPs rank, it is crucial to understand what it actually is? Basically, Alexa is a sort of new revolution among the marketers, as it is an intelligent personal assistant, which is developed by the Amazon to compare the popularity or rank of your website relative to other sites. It is very popular among the marketers for many years and results it provides help the marketers to know the online reputation of websites. It is intelligent assistance that keeps the data of a number of websites and ranks it as per their popularity. Now you know what it actually is, so, it's time to dig deeply into its importance. Let's get started.

It is a great measure to compare websites and is mainly used for assessing traffic, which is essential to increase the rate of conversion.

Your Google ranking can affect your Alexa Ranking; therefore, it is important for you to maintain your high position on the very first page to get expected outcomes of your efforts.

As it shows the ranking of your website as per its popularity, so, it makes it easier for you and other marketers to understand the actual potential of your company.

Also, increase in Alexa rank may put a positive impact on increasing the ranking of your website among different search engines, which automatically pull in the flood of traffic and increases the rate of conversion.

The Alexa Rank puts a very positive impact on your company and your brand among people and gives a boost to your credibility in the market.

It measures all the web pages and traffic on websites in the same way.

In short, it helps you understand where you actually stand in the market and where you need to reach. Also, from the above, it is clear why Alexa rank is important for your SERPs rank, so, you should pay attention to it. Though the task of improving your website rank on this popular intelligent personal assistance can be tedious, especially, if you are not aware of the marketing tactics. But the outcomes, it delivers at the end will take away all your stress and tiredness. Every marketer to make the distinct position of their company should invest their time and manpower in it and it will surely improve the rank and the conversion rate of your website

HOW TO CHOOSE THE BEST EARN MONEY ONLINE PROGRAM USING THE ALEXA RANKING TOOL

There are so many earn money online programs out there that it is very difficult to decide which one to choose and which ones actually work.

Make sure that the make money online program that you choose has the following to offer:

1-a money back guarantee

2- It is very important that the program offers learning methods on many ways on how to make money online.The aim is to be an online marketer and gradually develop towards a field which you find suits your needs and while doing so gain a vast knowledge on the Internet and its workings.

3-provides productivity tools, manuals, software and articles that are constantly maintained and updated.

4-provides practical tasks which you have to perform in the learning process

5-tutorials are based on first hand experience of the techniques involved

6-gives access to a blog with updates, advice, direction and tips

7-video tutorials. These are very easy to follow as they contain screenshots which makes learning faster.

8-offers you already set up money making websites that you can start earning from while you go about the process of learning how the Internet works.

9-do a search on "reviews money online program" and check out comments made by other individuals on the Net.Join a few forums if you have to,to gather more information. An example of a such forum is Work at Home Forum.com

10-Finally make sure that support is provided Once you have made a short list of the earn-money-online programs which fit the above criteria I would suggest running them through Alexa so you can finalise your decision. Alexa Ranking Tool. Alexa is a very powerful tool used to rank web site traffic. Find out how all the make money online programs rank compared to each other. This is one of the most accurate freely available tools to find out how well a site ranks up against millions of other sites on the Web.

Remember: The Alexa Ranking Tool also provides statistics as to which % of people from which countries are using this website.This further enhances the tool as you can see if people from your country are using this website which makes it more compatible to your individual needs. It has been noted that the Alexa Ranking Tool results is slightly skewed as it only measures visitors with the Alexa Toolbar installed,What needs to be further noted is that most webmasters have this toolbar installed and this is the quality traffic you actually need to measure for the above mentioned exercise.

These rankings are generally consistent with the amount of traffic they have.

NB: Should you decide to blog for money some paid blogging sites such as ReviewMe and Sponsored

Reviews are just three of the networks which base your ad selling strength on Alexa Ranks. To conclude bear in mind that despite the problems mentioned above with the Alexa Ranking Tool it is still the best way to check out rankings on the web.It is not 100% foolproof but will still give you the unfair advantage in getting that extra bit of information required before making an investment into the best earn-money-online program for you

HOW TO USE THE ALEXA TOOLBAR "SPARKY" FOR FIREFOX

So why is it important to add this to your firefox browser? Afterall don't we all have enough toolbars to fit 'up there.' Here are several reasons why you should consider using the Firefox toolbar as an serious internet marketer.

Like many handy toolbars there are two versions based on your preference in internet browsers. The Firefox toolbar is nicknamed "Sparky." If you're wondering the name originates from the traffic date "sparkline" which the toolbar places in the status bar. They exist primarily to provide a quick visual aid of the change in the website's Alexa rank over the previous three months.

The Alexa traffic rank sites right beside the sparkline, in addition to a bar giving the site's popularity in a visual depiction. The toolbar gives viewers the site's related sites after clicking anywhere on these features. This is great way to identify similar websites that may contain relevant content you need.

Another valuable reason to consider installing the toolbar is for your own ranking. It's well known that one of the primary means by which we recognize a site's popularity is by the Alexa score. However, a lot of marketers aren't aware that Alexa rank is based on how visitors who have the Alexa toolbar installed. So when you surf the internet with the toolbar installed you're passively casting votes for the visited sites, especially if you click on multiple pages within the site. This operates much like the Nielson ratings for television.

By now it should be obvious how the Alexa toolbar can play an invaluable time-saving role without taking up precious real estate. Follow the video in my blog post for step by step installation directions.

ALEXA RANKING VERSUS PAGERANK

For those that don't know what Page rank is, it is a number on a scale of 1 to 10, which should be thought of as the "trust" Google has in your website. There has been much debate on how important PR is to your websites success and search engine traffic.

Alexa ranking, on the other hand, is an altogether different number. Your Alexa rating is not determined by how much traffic your website receives, but rather the amount of visitors that reach your page that have the Alexa toolbar installed.

In my opinion you should be trying to improve your Alexa rating, but PR is a selling point for your website, should if you decide to sell or 'flip' your site on popular webmaster message boards.

The truth is, both PageRank and Alexa ranking improvements will be achieved by only by writing or creating quality content. Once you have done this, consider adding a vBulletin forum to your page, and let your community build links for your site through your own forums. Provide something new for your visitors, and let your ranking improve themselves. No magic formula here!

Using article websites as promotion is an excellent tactic for marketing your website, which can also be beneficial to your PR and Alexa rating. Not only do you get a high PR back link within your article, but you also will get potential clicks on this link, if your article is qualit

ALEXA RANK CHECKER - A RELIABLE TOOL TO FIND OUT YOUR WEBSITE'S PAGE RANK

If you are an online marketer and own a website, the performance of your site on the web matters a lot in the success of your business. It is important for every internet marketer to focus on a marketing strategy that helps to generate more traffic to the concerned website and accelerates the page rank in the various search engines.

The world of the internet and media is advancing fast, and the main concern of every digital marketer is to find out about the popularity of their website over the globe. The higher the popularity of a website, the better gets the ranking of the page. There are several kinds of online tools that help you determine the status of your site in a fraction of minutes.

Tools like Alexa Rank Checker or Google Page Rank Checker, are the legitimate means to cross check the performance of the site by entering the URL of the website. These are very simple to use and affordable at the same time. You can either use a free version or buy the paid versions for achieving better results.

The Alexa Rank checker is one of the most popular tools to find out about the traffic that your site is generating on a daily basis. This SEO tool is getting increasingly popular among the webmasters, search engine specialists and internet marketers because of the specialized plans and packages, the manufacturers of the tools have to offer their clients. It's affordable prices serve as an icing on the cake that is an excellent treat for the concerned group of people.

ALEXA PAGE RANKER- HOW DOES IT HELP TO CUT OFF MARKET COMPETITION?

The tool helps to track the SEO updates online. It provides an idea to the webmaster about the real position of their site, and they can think of the different ways to enhance their page ranking.

The tool is not only helpful in determining the Alexa page rank, but also help to figure out the Google page ranking of the website.

The broken backlinks can be thoroughly scrutinized and revised or replaced with the help of the tool as it helps in finding the perfect rank of the page.

How does it help with online marketing?

It is very important to understand the cut-throat competition in the way of the digital marketers and either the free version or the paid one of the same helps in facilitating the marketing campaign according to the need of the market.

Needless to say, it helps in strengthening the SEO tools and enhance the marketing strategy.

The Alexa ranking system is one of the new ranking systems of concern to anyone who is interested in improving traffic to their website. Alexa is owned by Amazon.com and ranks websites based on the amount of traffic to the website over the past three months. However, the rankings through Alexa are somewhat skewed because the information for a particular website is tracked through visitors who have the Alexa toolbar installed. This means there may be websites which get an exorbitant amount of traffic, but if they do not have a large number of visitors utilising the Alexa toolbar, their Alexa ranking will suffer.

Whether or not you decide to make a concerted effort to increase the Alexa ranking of your website is a personal decision you will have to make. Some website owners look at the popularity of Alexa with respect to Google and decide it is just not worth the effort.They figure they are getting enough traffic just by optimising for Google, so why invest the extra time and energy to increase their Alexa ranking as well. This is certainly understandable; however, it also should be noted a higher ranking on Alexa will certainly not detract from your success with Google or other search engines. It can only add more profit to your bottom line, so why not do what you can to increase your Alexa rank.

So just how do you increase an Alexa rank? If you are optimising for popular search engines, you are already headed down the right path because traffic plays the primary role in Alexa rankings. Make sure you are using the Alexa toolbar yourself. This is important because, as we mentioned previously, only visits from users who have the Alexa toolbar installed will be recorded. Next, add an Alexa rank widget to your website. You will get credit for a visit each time a user clicks on the widget and you may also be introducing some of your regular visitors to Alexa.

Tailor your content to entice those who are likely to have the Alexa toolbar installed to visit your website. The Alexa ranking is an important area of interest for many website owners, so many website owners will have the Alexa toolbar installed. Therefore, writing top quality content on subjects such as SEO, improving page rank and improving traffic, will likely bring visitors who have this toolbar installed. Likewise you can create a section of tools for website owners to bring this target audience to your website

If you are serious about building your online credibility and attracting more advertisers, you need to boost your Alexa rank.Alexa is a global benchmark of website popularity.It's now possible to do this by buying Alexa traffic.

But first, why is Alexa ranking so important?

Alexa remains a widely used reference in the internet marketing industry. Alexa is a ranking system that audits the number of visitors going to various websites with particular tracking attention given to those visitors with Alexa's toolbar installed. The system then generates a traffic rank, which shows the public how your website fares compared to millions of others in your country and around the world.

Here's the simple truth: Your Alexa rank allows advertisers to assess your marketing potential. The better your rank, the more popular your website is perceived to be-and the higher advertisers will pay for your ad space.

How to Improve Your Alexa Ranking

There are various methods that can be used to boost your Alexa traffic ranking, however all require distinct dedication, time and a strategic approach with a focus on increasing traffic.

1. Install the Alexa toolbar on your browser, and make your website your home page, so that every time you open your browser, you technically 'visit' your own site.

2. People with Alexa toolbars are web masters and internet marketers themselves. To attract these people to your site, you can post useful high-quality content that appeals to them. Promote your page on popular webmaster forums and social networking sites like digg.com, StumbleUpon, and del.icio.us.

You should also make sure to have your website's URL on your signature whenever you post on internet marketing forums.

3. Write informative blogs about Alexa. This will help you attract visitors who are themselves more likely to have the Alexa toolbars installed and are looking to improve their rank, just like you are.

Buying Alexa Traffic

While the above methods work, they take a significant time to improve your Alexa rank. Luckily there's a faster and more efficient way to boost your ranking within a few weeks-and that is to buy Alexa traffic. Buying Alexa traffic allows you to gain status, authority, and credibility, ultimately giving you the power to command top dollar from advertisers

CHAPTER NINE

IMPROVE YOUR ALEXA RANKING

Why should you improve your Alexa ranking? Well, there are several reasons! Whether you operate an e-commerce site that sells products or services online or a small content-driven blog, you can greatly enhance your site's traffic and earnings if you increase your Alexa ranking. To know more about how and why any website stands to gain from this, read below.

Alexa Internet Inc. is an internet services provider founded in 1996. It runs the ultra-popular and famous Alexa web-ranking technology that has come to be used by millions of companies and individuals worldwide as a sort of who's who guide to the World Wide Web. Even giant search corporations, such as Google and Yahoo, often use a site's Alexa score as an index of its importance on the web.

The Internet has radically simplified global trade. The flip side, however, is that it is now easier for criminals to steal your money. Cyber crime is constantly increasing, with thousands of phishing and scam sites trying to steal people's information and money. In such a scenario, users are increasingly becoming choosy about sites with whom they want to do business- and rightly so!

Naturally, everybody prefers to deal with the most trusted sites. On the Internet, highly ranked and highly visited equates to trustworthy. Interestingly, these two criteria are interlinked. If you get one the other one automatically follows.

For online merchants, it's important to demonstrate reliability to customers. One way of doing this is to improve your Alexa ranking. A good Alexa position reassures people that your site has a vast number of visitors, which, in turn, communicates that it is secure and reliable.

As mentioned earlier, an improved position automatically attracts a large numbers of users. This in itself is better for business, since more visitors always translate to more sales. Besides, Alexa is a highly useful site statistics analysis tool. It provides valuable insights into how your business stacks up to the competition and how to improve your SEO efforts.

Even if you operate a non-commercial site, it's a good idea to improve your Alexa ranking to increase advertising revenue. Advertisers universally use Alexa to check how much traffic a site has to assess its marketing potential and how much to bid for ad space.

A rank less than 100,000 is considered somewhat well traveled. Less than 50,000 is popular, while lower than 10,000 and 1,000 ultra-visited and web-elite, respectively.

There are a variety of service providers and companies out there that offer to enhance your site's

Alexa ranking. However, they prove effective in some aspects - while some work, others do not. A good way of determining how reliable a company is and whether they will deliver on their claims is to look for a money-back guarantee.

Under such a program, the company guarantees to return all your money if it fails to improve your Alexa ranking to your desired and pre-determined position, with the promised period of time.

5 Important Things to Remember When Purchasing Internet Marketing Software

Oh I do realise that most Internet marketing software websites offer you an iron-clad 100% money back guarantee if you are not completely satisfied with their products, but going through the process of claiming back a refund is often not as easy as they make out. It's better to try to avoid purchasing products that are useless in the first place. So here are 5 simple guidelines to remember each time you purchase any Internet marketing software products, which if implemented, will help you to avoid any disappointment and save you the trouble of claiming back refunds for your products.

1. If you are considering purchasing any Internet marketing software products, you should always read the sales page thoroughly and read it more than once! Don't speed read through, just reading what you want to read.. You must establish exactly what the vendor is claiming the software will do. You are also advised to carry out a Google search for a review of this Internet marketing software and find out what those who have used the product are saying about it.

2. If the vendor is suggesting in the sales page that this particular piece of Internet marketing software requires regular use for a certain period of time before reasonable results can be expected, then make sure that the guarantee period offered on the product, is longer than the trial period.

3. A good test I often implement when buying any marketing software, is to take a good look at the vendor websites' performance through the Alexa.com website. For example, if the sales page is selling Traffic Software, then you would naturally assume that the vendor would have used his own software on his own sites, and therefore his sales page should show some decent traffic results on Alexa, if the traffic software is useful at all. Similarly, if the piece of Internet marketing software in question, is designed to bring lots of incoming backlinks to your website, then check the sales page for backlinks. If the software really works you will see good backlink results in the vendor's website.

4. Don't be fooled by time-sensitive offers. I find them so annoying. As with any Internet marketing software offer, the price will be the same tomorrow..and the day after.. and probably the day after that! Take your time in making your decisions. Remember that if a vendor lowers the price on any product, it is usually because he is struggling to sell it

at it's original price. No sensible vendor would drop the price if the product was selling well at the original price!

5. Now let's discuss guarantees for a moment. Most software products will be offered with a guarantee which is typically between 60 and 90 days. The vendor will often use the offer of a guarantee as part of his sales pitch, and this ploy is designed to allay any fears you may have about the risk involved in buying their Internet marketing software product. But they have in mind that 60 or 90 days down the line you may well have forgotten about claiming your money back on any unsatisfactory items. By this time you have moved on to something new and probably can't be concerned with the guarantee claim process. When you purchase any Internet marketing software product, make a note in your diary a couple of days before the guarantee period is set to lapse and when you get to that date, if you were dissatisfied with the results, then claim your money back immediately.

Most Internet marketers who have been working online for any length of time will no doubt have a whole stack of Internet marketing software items on their PC that they never use, purely because they know the products just dont produce the necessary results. Sometimes the collective cost of these items can represent thousands of dollars being spent unnecessarily. So if you follow these 5 simple guidelines when you buy any Internet marketing software tools, you are extremely likely to reduce the amount of 'unwanted software' in your PC

Why It's Important To Have A High Quality WebsiteQuality Content

Only when a website has quality content, can it reach its full potential. The first advantage is obvious, because the content of a website is the basis for its search engine ranking. When evaluating a website, both the quality and the quantity of website content play a prominent role. Yet, even if the quantity is lacking but the quality is there, you still drive more traffic to your website than if things were the other way around. Quality content makes sense, is informative, serves a purpose and is relevant. Overuse of keywords, blabbering for the sake of quantity of words, and talking about irrelevant facts that are useless to the viewers targeted are all considered low quality content.

If you do not have the ability to create the quality content needed to make a high quality website, it's worth every penny to simply hire a professional web design company!

Better a lot of money for a lot of results, than a little money with no result!

It's always best to buy a professional website design with search engine optimized coding. Meaning it's mobile responsive, modern and clean in code design.

The amount of content is another significant factor in high quality website design.

The more QUALITY content, the better

Extensive content allows your website to be an extensive field of action. Various relevant topics are covered and this gives search engines a real party. An analysis of strong search phrases, keywords and covering prominent subjects would help with appearing in best ranking tools such as Alexa. Good and worthy content attracts potential customers and as a result of that quality content, they not only stay on your site, but they are more likely to come back and perform the desired action (such as make a purchase).

A high quality website increases the probability for visitors spending a large amount of time on your site. Retention of users on the site is an important feature when considering global ranking. With good rankings on Google you can be more visible to your target audience, while your quality content is shared amongst its readers bringing you even more exposure and business.

Another important factor in professional web design is uniqueness!

Great features, new readers

With a professional, unique website, you can stand out from the crowd and be competitive in the online world. Ruminate not to publish a website which already exists elsewhere - aim to create and innovate the building of a custom design. A unique style is refreshing to your visitors. Create a unique website with cool features like blogs or discussion boards. All of these benefits apply to private websites, as well as commercial.

What's another thing that high quality websites do?

Make use of the time!

Use your website content to connect with your readers and show your expertise!

Trust is something that is very important in the world of online business. People do not make impulse purchases like they once did online without looking at the website ranking, relevance of content and expertise. The game has changed from the time when people could have outdated websites with little or no social networking. Today's online business is all about promotion of better products and services. And better promotion means who knows the most about what they are selling!

If you cannot bring all these components to your website, it is useless to build one!

Why hire professionals to build your website and spend extra money?

Professional web designers think big. They create a visual language for the brand to be consistent in different contexts.Your website, logo, business cards and even your Twitter profile and Facebook have to be created in a way to a have a consistency and coherence. Brands that have a consistent visual language make it a memorable impression in the minds of the customers. And professional web designers are going to give you a finished product that is high quality internally and externally as both are equally important.

You may be an expert in your business, but you may not be an expert in quality website creation. Sometimes there needs to be a compromise between what price you want and what works for the web. Quality web design also comes from the experience of knowing how to translate ideas into web pages. Quality design takes all your unique selling points and turns them into a consistent visual message. The choice of font, text spacing, and contrast are the details that make a difference in the overall quality of your site.

SEO Analysis - Some Important Tools

The visibility and position of our website is very important to our business and so, we need to make sure that our optimization efforts are successful. We need to constantly monitor the progress of our site and determine the loopholes or errors which can affect the overall ranking or positioning of our site. Thus, SEO analysis in an important aspect in the process of optimizing a website and there are quite a few tools available in the market, which can help us in this process.

Here is a list of few more SEO analysis tools that people can use:

1) Rank Checker - This is a very simple tool that can be added as a Firefox extension or plug-in. While browsing the internet, you can run this tool and it will check your website for positioning related data. It will then create a report which will include data about different aspects of your site. However, some people have questioned the reliability of this data. It is a free tool and so there is nothing much to complain about.

2) Popuri - This tool blends a lot of information into one report and it provides information about Page Rank as per Alexa, Rankeo and other sites. It also tells you about Del.icio.us links, links reported by Yahoo and more.It calculates the overall popularity of the site based on these different parameters.

3) Raven - It is one of the tools, which has become popular over a period of time and it gives you a score of your site, which is obtained from SEO analysis of your site based on its content, the usage of tags, etc. It is a good tool to understand the overall performance of the website.

4) SEO Grader - Another great tool which can be utilized to obtain a complete SEO report of your site. It helps in finding the status of your page in different search engines like Google, Bing, Yahoo etc., indexed pages, level of traffic, and appearances in Dmoz as well as other directories etc.

5) SEO-Centro - This is a useful tool for SEO analysis which gives you a good idea about the keyword density in your site. Based on its report, one can determine the usage of important keywords and improve the optimization of the site, based on those keywords. It also helps in checking ranks, analyzing Meta Tags, determining popularity of links and even suggests keywords for the site.

CHAPTER TEN

HOW IMPORTANT ARE THESE WEB TRAFFIC
RANKINGS?

You may have heard experts say before that
traffic is one of the most important things you have
to work hard for if you want to make money online.
This is mostly because without it, you won't get the
visitors who can be your potential clients and
customers. Not having these prospects is a bad thing
for your venture, so you really have to take the
measures that can help you generate the amount of
traffic you need.

But what are these web traffic rankings and why
are they so important?

Web traffic rankings, in the simplest of sense, are
the statistics specific companies and search engines
formulate to determine which sites come first in the
list of search results. You may know them as Google
or Alexa page ranks. Normally, your site can be

ranked from 1 to 10 or 1 to 5. The higher your ranking is, the better chances you have in showing up in the first page of the search results.

Why is it so important that you get high rankings? It's simple. People today have arguably short attention spans. So, if your site doesn't pop out the first page in their searches, there's a big chance that your site won't be found and visited. Of course, this isn't a very good thing if you're aiming for the big time, so you will have to take measures to improve your standing.

This is why you should take the appropriate steps to improve your web traffic rankings. Luckily, that can be done by making your web presence more felt by the public through a variety of ways. For one, you can get your site listed in different directories and social bookmarking websites. You can also gain a lot from leaving a link to your site in different blogs and forum communities that search engines index and crawl into.

Seriously, there are tons of ways you can help yourself and your site to get higher website traffic rankings. You just need to know the right techniques and tricks to succeed in this venture.

SOME OTHER IMPORTANT INSTRUCTIONS FOR QUALITY LINK BUILDING

Local & Business Links

1. Try to get the links from local sites which are based on same theme.

2. Join the better communities related to your business.

3. Try to submit your site link in different relevant city and state government resources.

4. Submit your site in the local library's website.

5. Find if your retailers or other business partners who may be link to your site.

6. Improve the business relationships with others who are not your competitors. You can do this by

sharing the links, business ideas and business cards also.

7. Introduce an affiliate program also so that many people will link your site who takes your affiliation.

Easy Free Links

8. Submit your site on different free classified sites depending on your category.

9. Participate in different answer and questions on different sites like yahoo, wiki etc which provide facility to add links to relevant resource.

10. Participate in answer and questions on Google Groups which allows you to add related site links.

11. Create your company page in Wikipedia or in topic specific wikis. If you are not able to add your link directly then add the other page link which directly link to your site.

12. Create a Squidoo page in such a manner that it should look like an industry expert. You cannot link your site only there so try to link related product and tools also.

13. Submit your site story on Digg that links to your site article.

14. If you have useful content and update it frequently then create an RSS feed because some people can syndicate your RSS content.

15. Mostly all forums allow member to add links in their signature so you will see your site link in each post automatically.

Post the Reviews about different products

16. Most of the brands are not well established on the web so if you post a good review about their products then it is possible that your review will rank well.

17. Post your review on related products on Amazon, you will get direct enquiries from there.

18. Use Amazon to create list of top product as your review and you can mention your site link in background.

19. Use Alexa to review other sites, your site will be listed in related traffic streams.

20. Review different products on different shopping sites which you can find on shopping search engines like ePinions.

21. If you purchase a product or service then there is an option to leave your review or testimonial, you can leave your link at many places.

Blogs & the Blogosphere

22. Create a blog and post their good quality content regularly. Leave your site link in the post but don't spam there.

23. Link some other related blogs also from your blog because if they get any visitor from your blog then they will noticed about your blog. It is an easy way to get noticed.

24. Comment on different other blogs because there is an option to leave your site link. If you have commented on relevant blogs and if webmaster approves it then you will get a quality link from that blog. This link may be count as your site back-link

and if not then other blogger will notice about your site at least.

25. Crate pages on Technorati because pages on this site rank well in major search engines.

26. If you have a blog then you should submit in some quality blog directories.

Important Issues to Remember Before Buying an Expired Domain Name

Buying expired domains is a tricky topic! You will need to be very careful while buying an expired domain because many of these domains may have some problems associated with their registration. There have been instances when the previous owner decided to approach the legal authorities to reclaim their expired domains. While you need to be very careful in your dealings, you may also need to consider the following issues before buying domains that are expiring.

The issue of domain trademark: Make sure that the domain that you buy does not have any trademark associated with it. You will need to be very careful in dealing with domains that have trademarks against their URL. You could even land in potential legal hassles when you buy such domains. You may wish to conduct a detailed research to check whether the domain expired has any trademark. Use one of the web sites that provide information on trademarks.

The issue of corporate expired domain names: Many domain names have a close relation with corporate businesses. If a company or a business firm owns the domain names, you may even forfeit such domain names. In some instances, companies may simply forget to renew some of their domain names.

Tip: It is almost difficult to find out who is the real owner of a domain name before it expired. However, you can still find out more about a particular expired domain name.

To find out more about expired domains and their previous ownership, use these tools to conduct a detailed research:

a) Go to alexa that maintains a big database of millions of web sites. You can find out details like link popularity, ownership, traffic, ratings or rankings etc in this exhaustive web site. Some times, you may never find any information on some of the domain names.

b) Go to Google to check the cache status of the expired domain names. Google always maintains a cache directory of web sites by using its spider technology. It is possible to visit a cached online copy of a web domain, including expired ones. With this tool, you can find out if the expired domain you want to buy had any trademark associated with it. Type the URL of the expired domain into the Google search engine box and make sure that you are checking the cache copy of the expired web domain.

c) Use link popularity checking tools: You can find out more about previously owned expired domains. Choose any of the link popularity checking web sites and enter the URL of the expired domain to check the links against the name. This gives you a fair estimate of the number of online references related to the domains. Zero values mean that the domain expired did not have any activity while higher values signify that the domain was very active in its previous avatar. However, the downside of this method is that you may find it very difficult to find the quality of these links. Some domains may have just a few links associated with it. However, these links may be very good in that they came from high quality web sites. On the other hand, an expired domain may have lot of links that came from insignificant web domains. Making a comparison just on the number of links may be quite premature and improper.

By using the above mentioned tools, you can find out minute and precise information about your expired domain. However, use these tools with utmost caution and without any prejudice as some of the data extracted could be misleading

Link Building So As to Have Good Page Rank and Alexa Rank

Search engines currently base relevancy primarily on linkage patterns. Who links to you and how they link to you are what determines where your site will rank for competitive search queries.

Few steps for Link Building:-

1) Make sure your site has something that other webmasters in your niche would be interested in linking to.

2) When possible, get your keywords in the link text pointing to your site.

3) Register with, participate in, or trade links with topical hubs and related sites. Be in the discussion or at least be near the discussion.

4) Look for places to get free links from.

5) Produce articles and get them syndicated.

6) Participate in forums to learn about what your potential consumers think is important.

7) Issue press releases with links to your site.

8) Leave super glowing testimonials for people and products you really like.

9) Leave relevant comments in blogs that do not send their comments through redirects.

10) Sponsor charities, blogs, or web sites related to your site.

11) Consider renting links if you are in an extremely competitive industry.

12) Mix your link text up, if you can.

13) Survey your vertical and related verticals. What ideas/tools/articles have become industry standard tools or well-cited information?What ideas are missing?

14)All the links pointing to your site should not have the same exact link text as that could be a sure sign of link spamming. You want to mix it up and use different text links from different sites. This will make it appear as natural linking to search engines.

Link placements - how often and how fast how to determine the actual value of your website this is the main key to find the info about any website in affects with any of its technical prospect, all you require to do is to put the name of that very website about which you desire to collect information into its search engine and then you will be having various kind of information about that peculiar website on your finger tips. You have a website that you like to sell but you do not know how much to deal it for. How do you ascertain the value of a website and what the selling price would be? How often is your website worth?

To you, your Website is worth or values more than it is to somebody else.That is because of sentimental reasons.It's your Website.You made it.You see it otherwise than others do. But, you require determining how much somebody else would purchase it for and you require doing that objectively.

Here are some metrics that you can utilize to value your Website:

Age of the domain - Older Domains commonly ranking amend in Search Engines.The much older your domain, the more and more your Website is worth.

Google Page Rank - The much higher your Google Page Rank, the more amazing Google thinks your Website is. As Google is the greatest Search Engine, your Website is worth more if Google conceives it to be important.

Alexa Traffic Rank - Alexa ranks all Websites on the Internet. The more advanced your Website's Alexa ranking, the advanced it's imagined traffic. Alexa is not totally accurate but without access to genuine traffic data, it is what most of the people use to estimate a Website's traffic.

The amount of indexed pages - The more and more pages indexed by Search Engines, the more likely traffic from a diversity of different keywords.

Total number of links - The more links that charge to a Website, the more dealings it could accept from disparate sources.Business directories are a best source of links.

The above are simple minded metrics, as utilized by dnScoop ascertain the value of a Website. Of course, there are lot other factors that will determine how much a purchaser is wishing to pay, letting in the potential of enhanced traffic in the future and whether or not the Website really earns any revenue.

Link Placements - How Often and How Fast

When you first start submitting articles or links to article and directory sites, you need to make sure that you don't over do it. Even if you have great content, and your site is 100% legitimate, the speed at which you submit your articles and links can get you filtered out as search engine spam.

Below I've outlined a process to effectively and efficiently submit your articles and links and stay on good terms with article and directory site owners.

Before You Submit

Instead of trying to find submission sites on-the-fly, it's much more efficient to do your homework first. You need to gather your resources, determine where you want to submit, and compile your list.

How you do this? First, if you're submitting articles, my rule of thumb is to find article directories with a PageRank of at least four. It's okay to submit to lower page rank directories, just make sure they're legitimate. Also, you might want to check out the Alexa rating for the sites you're submitting to. One way to detect a possible link farm is to look at the site's Alexa rating and compare it with its PageRank. If the Alexa rating is high (not as good) but the

PageRank is high, then you know something is awry. If a site has a high PageRank it should also have a lower (better) Alexa rating.

Check the site's cache in Google. Has it been awhile since Google has been around? It's probably not a trusted site. Does the cache show a different site? Could be a PageRank redirect site.Avoid these at all costs.

Some common, high PageRank article directories include EzineArticles.com, goarticles.com, and isnare.com. I don't recommend signing up for article distribution services. You have no control over where your article goes if you submit to these sites. All it takes is one article on a spam site to ruin your reputation.

Your Submission "Speed"

I recommend that you submit one article at a time to at least 10 different directories. Don't submit all the articles you've written to one site at a single time. By the time you've finished submitting one article to 10 different sites, you can go back and submit your other articles, moving down the list as you complete each one.

Make certain you read and understand the terms of service and submission guidelines for each article or link directory that you submit to. Some article directories only allow a few submissions per day. You need to adhere to the submission guidelines. It's much better to be able to submit fewer articles per day than to do a massive submission and risk getting your articles deleted, or worse, losing your account.

After you've submitted to the first 10 directories, find 10 additional directories to submit to. Repeat the process I described above. Use should not submit a single article or link to more than 50 directories per day.

Maintain a Clean Submission Process

Your article and link submission process is a very important part of your linking strategy. You have to make sure that you understand what the directories want and that you follow their rules. You may think the rules are stiff, but it actually helps maintain a clean community.

Because of the proliferation of mass submission software, commonly used by those webmasters who are trying to make a quick buck, submission sites have come down hard on anyone who even hints of being a spammer. If you submit too fast to too many directories, I can guarantee that you will be labeled a spammer and your articles, or links, will be deleted.

MOTORING YOUR WEBSITE

The site traffic is an important statistic to measure. If you are just interested in where your website appears on the search engine rankings for a given keyword without considering the visitors coming into your website as a result of those keyword rankings then you will be flying blind.

Most ecommerce hosting providers will offer webstats to their customers, usually at no extra charge. There are two types of website monitoring to choose from.

First, a log file analyzer such as "Urchin" which is paid or the free "AWStats" used by business first can be considered. These are installed on the server that is hosting your ecommerce website. If the referrer option is turned on then you will be able to see from which website the visitor had come from. Log file analysers process visitor statistics in batch rather than in real time which leads to the next option.

A real time browser based tracking such as "WebStat" can be used which involves inserting a javascript tracking code or image on each page of the site that is to be monitored. Each time a page is loaded then that code will be able to update the statistics of that page and thereby providing real time information. Real time statistics tend to be more expensive than log file analysers.

The important metrics to measure when monitoring your website are as follows.

1) Keywords that visitors have typed into search engines to find your site should be checked regularly. You may be able to find unexpected keyword combinations that people have used to find your site which you could then focus on. If most visitors are using keywords that you are trying to promote, then that is a measure of success of your internet marketing campaign. If most visitors are using keywords that you are not trying to promote then you have chosen the wrong keywords and need to modify your campaign accordingly.

2) The search engine that people use to find your site can be tracked. Google will be the top of the list but you may find users that make use of specialist search engines that you may not have considered previously.

3) Referrals are the tracking of the actual websites that brought traffic to your site. From this you will be able to see the amount of traffic that you get from websites that refer to your site. Sometimes people type in your address directly into the address bar and these visitors are registered as "no referral" or "direct" entries. A technique to determine which visitors are typing in your address into the address bar, and which visitors have bookmarked your site is to use an icon file with your site which is displayed in the bookmarks menu as an image. Favicons are also useful for branding your business. You will then be able to check your server logs for fetches to this icon file which indicates approximately how many people have bookmarked your site.

3)The number of page views can be used to determine the most popular pages of your site. You will then be able to focus more effort to the pages that are less popular.

4) Visitor path is the route your visitors take when navigating your site. This can be helpful to show what visitors are usually looking for when they enter your site and can help diagnose navigational deficiencies.

5) Exit pages are the pages that people are looking at before they leave your website. Usually this will be the shopping cart software on your ecommerce website after they have made a purchase, assuming that your site has high conversion rate.

6) The length of time people spend on your site and on individual pages can be used to check if people are actually reading what is on a page or if that page's content is deficient so that people do not spend time reading the content. A short length of session should be addressed by improving the content of your site.

The importance of monitoring your website is to increase the chance of visitors purchasing a product from your ecommerce website. If you spend all your time making sure your website ranks on the first page of goggle without considering the above metrics, then you may end up with a good ranking but low conversion ratio. Nevertheless, rankings are important because if a customer cannot find your site. If you use the services of an SEO company, they must provide you with regular reports on your keyword rankings. You may also want to manually check the pagerank of your site. Webstatistics software do not usually provide pagerank information although you can download the Google toolbar to view pagerank information or you can download the Alexa toolbar to view your Alexa rankings.

90407600R00078

Made in the USA
Columbia, SC
02 March 2018